Bedroom Makeover Crafts

KATHY ROSS

ILLUSTRATED BY NICOLE in den BOSCH

M Millbrook Press/Minneapolis

For Beverly and the rooms we furnish!

—KR

Text copyright © 2009 by Kathy Ross
Illustrations copyright © 2009 by Lerner Publishing Group, Inc.

Millbrook Press
A division of Lerner Publishing Group, Inc.
241 First Avenue North
Minneapolis, MN 55401 U.S.A.

Website address: www.lernerbooks.com

Library of Congress Cataloging-in-Publication Data
Ross, Kathy (Katharine Reynolds), 1948–
   Bedroom Makeover Crafts / by Kathy Ross ; illustrated by Nicole in den Bosch.
      p.   cm. — (Girl crafts)
   ISBN: 978–0–8225–7593–1 (lib. bdg. : alk. paper)
   1. Handicraft for girls—Juvenile literature. 2. Girls' bedrooms—Juvenile literature. I. Bosch, Nicole in den. II. Title.
TT171.R72 2009
745.5083—dc22   2007001894

Manufactured in the United States of America
1 2 3 4 5 6 – PA – 14 13 12 11 10 09

Contents

Tuck your mementoes in a work of art!

Web Holder

Here is what you need:

ruler

scissors

pony bead

white craft glue

4 or more kinds of yarn, such as eyelash or pom-pom

wire coat hanger

Here is what you do:

1. Pull the center of the bottom of the wire hanger down to form a diamond shape.

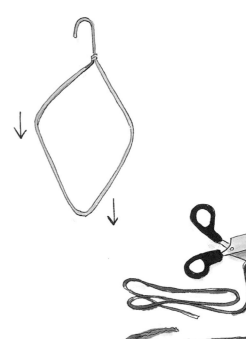

2. Cut a 5-foot (152.5-cm) piece from each of the different kinds of yarn.

3. Tie the end of one piece of yarn to the neck of the hanger. Then cross it to the bottom. Wrap it around the edge. Continue crisscrossing the yarn across the hanger at different angles.

4. When you have about 2 inches (5 cm) left, tie off the end of the yarn on the edge of the hanger. Trim the ends.

5. Use the other pieces of yarn in the same way to create a web across the hanger.

6. Cut a 2-foot (61-cm) piece of one of the thicker yarns. Use it to wrap the hook. Tie off each end to secure. Trim ends.

7. Glue the pony bead on the end of the hook.

Hang the web by the hook. Display photos, notes, and other paper keepsakes by tucking them into the yarn web.

Make pretty display boxes for small figurines and other treasures.

Treasure Shelf

Here is what you need:

small jewelry box tops and bottoms

printed papers, such as wrapping or scrapbook paper

large box bottom, 2 inches (5 cm) deep

collage materials, such as small flowers and bows

scissors

paint and a paintbrush

thin ribbon

white craft glue

newspaper

Here is what you do:

1. Place the smaller boxes inside the large box to create several display compartments. Cut off pieces of the sides to make the boxes fit together.

2. When you are happy with the arrangement, glue the boxes in place.

3. Working on the newspaper, paint the inside and edges of the shelf. Let dry.

4. Line the backs of some or all the sections with printed paper. Glue down the paper. Let dry.

5. Glue small bows, flowers, or other collage items in the corners of some of the boxes.

6. Tie a piece of the thin ribbon in a bow around the box.

Stand the box on your dresser or a shelf, and fill it with figurines and other small treasures. If you wish to hang the box, glue the two ends of a 6-inch (15-cm) ribbon to each side of the back to make a hanger.

Store those special cards and letters in style!

Heart Letter Holder

Here is what you need:

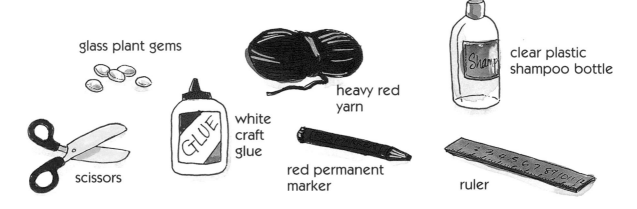

glass plant gems

heavy red yarn

clear plastic shampoo bottle

white craft glue

scissors

red permanent marker

ruler

Here is what you do:

1. Cut the bottle in half. Discard the top half.

2. Use the marker to sketch a 4-inch (10-cm) heart shape on the front of the bottle.

3. Cut ½ inch (1.3 cm) down from the top. Then cut all the way around the bottle. Cut around the top of the heart. Cut a slat, 1 inch wide by 2 inches deep (2.5 by 5 cm) on either side.

4. Use the permanent marker to color the heart red.

5. Cut a cupful of snips of the red yarn.

6. Cover the heart shape with glue. Press the snips into the glue.

7. Glue the gems on the inside of the bottom of the bottle to weigh it down.

You can also jazz up the heart with glitter, beads, ribbon, and other fun decorations.

This earring holder is a real doll!

Earring Doll

Here is what you need:

2½-inch (6.4-cm) Styrofoam ball

2 12-inch (30.5-cm) pipe cleaners

large mesh bath scrubby

curly ribbon package bow

3 pony beads

pencil

white craft glue

2 heart-shaped beads

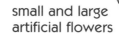

small and large artificial flowers

Here is what you do:

1. Poke the pencil all the way through the center of the Styrofoam ball to make a hole.

10

2. Slide the ball onto the rope holder of the scrubby. The ball will be the head.

3. Wrap the center of a pipe cleaner around the rope below the head so the pipe cleaner becomes the arms.

4. String the second pipe cleaner through the string tie at the bottom of the scrubby so the pipe cleaner becomes the legs.

5. Glue curly ribbon bow to the top of the head for hair.

6. Glue the pony beads to the front of the head for the eyes and mouth. Lightly press them into the foam.

(continued on next page)

7. Glue and press the heart beads into the head for cheeks.

8. Pull the artificial flowers apart to separate the petal layers.

9. Slide two large petal layers over the rope at the top of the doll. Secure the flower hat with glue.

10. Slide a small petal over the end of each arm and leg. Fold over 1 inch (2.5 cm) of the pipe cleaner ends to shape the hands and feet.

Attach pairs of earrings through the mesh body to keep them from getting lost.

Decorate your doorknob!

Doorknob Posy

Here is what you need:

2 green small ponytail bands

12-inch (30-cm) green pipe cleaner

9 small ponytail bands in different colors

Here is what you do:

1. Start with a band for the flower center. (Be sure not to use the two green bands.)

2. Thread a second band through itself around the flower center to make a flower petal.

3. Make seven more petals.

4. Fold the pipe cleaner in half over the flower center. Twist the ends together to form a stem.

5. Thread the two green bands through themselves on the stem to form two leaves.

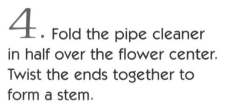

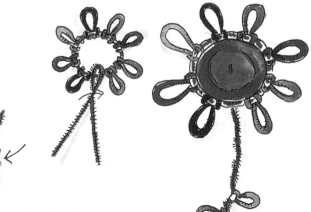

Slip the flower over a doorknob so that the knob becomes the center of the flower. Cute!

This project is a pretty way to protect your small dolls
and other treasures from dust.

Doll Bubble

Here is what you need:

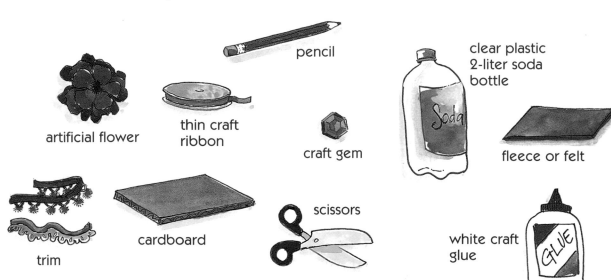

pencil

artificial flower

thin craft
ribbon

craft gem

clear plastic
2-liter soda
bottle

fleece or felt

trim

cardboard

scissors

white craft
glue

Here is what you do:

1. Remove the label, and cut
the spout end off the bottle.

2. Trace around the open end
on the cardboard. Cut out the circle.
In the same way, cut a circle from the
fleece or felt.

3. Glue the fleece or felt circle to the cardboard.

4. Glue trim around the cut base of the bubble. Turn the cut bottle over so that the bottom becomes the top of the bubble.

5. Pull the artificial flower apart. Glue two layers of the petals to each other. Glue the craft gem in the center. This is the flower.

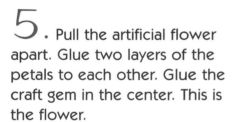

6. Tie two pieces of ribbon into a bow. Glue the bow to the top of the bubble. Glue the flower on top of the bow.

Stand a small doll or figurine on the cardboard circle and cover it with the decorated bubble. You can make several of these using different size bottles and different trims.

Keep track of small items with these fancy boxes.

Dresser Boxes

Here is what you need:

one large and one small cardboard frozen juice can with metal ends

white craft glue

ribbons

artificial flowers

craft gems

newspaper

paints and a paintbrush

scissors

Here is what you do:

1. Clean and dry the juice cans. Cut the top portion off each juice can. Save the metal lids from the cut portions.

2. Working on the newspaper, paint the containers inside and outside. Paint both sides of the lids. Let dry.

3. Glue ribbons around the outside of the two containers.

4. Pull the artificial flowers apart. Glue two or three layers of petals to the top of each lid. Glue a craft gem in the center.

You can dress up your dresser by making many of these boxes in different heights and colors.

Stash special notes from friends or your latest report card
in this handy organizer.

Pocket Board

Here is what you need:

cardboard, 11 by 12 inches
(27.5 by 30 cm)

scissors

white craft glue

glass jelly jar

fabric

ruler

trim

clear packing
tape

felt

Here is what you do:

1. Cover the front of the cardboard by wrapping it with a piece of the fabric. Glue the edges to the back of the cardboard.

2. Fold over the top edge of a second piece of fabric. Place the fabric on the front of the board, 3 inches (8 cm) from the top. Glue the excess fabric to the back of the board.

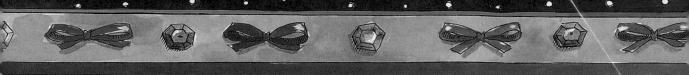

3. Add a second fabric pocket 3 inches (8 cm) below the first. Add a third pocket.

4. Glue a piece of felt to the back of the pocket board.

5. Glue trim across the top edge of each pocket.

6. Glue the glass jar to the back of the bottom of the pocket board to make it stand. Secure the jar with a strip of the clear packing tape.

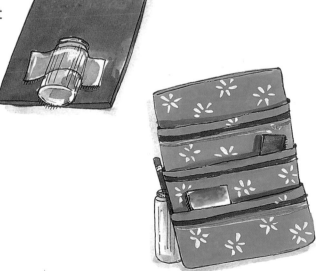

You can stash bigger pieces of paper in the top pocket. Medium-size papers go in the middle pocket. Small notes can be stored in the bottom pocket. Put pencils and note paper in the jar behind the pocket board.

This calendar will never be outdated!
Just flip to the correct day, month, and date.

Perpetual Calendar

Here is what you need:

white craft
glue

4 by 6-inch (10 by
15-cm) 40-page
spiral notebook

markers

colored and
printed paper

old photos or
copies of photos

collage materials,
such as ribbon, gems,
stickers, sequins

cardboard

pen

ruler

scissors

old greeting cards

Here is what you do:

1. Turn the notebook on its side with the spiral at the top.

2. Cut 31 pages of the notebook into three sections. The first section should be 2 inches (5 cm) wide, the second 2½ inches (6.3 cm) wide, and the third 1½ inches (3.8 cm) wide.

3. Cover seven pages in the first section with colored or printed paper. Beginning with Sunday, write the days of the week at the top of each page. Decorate each page.

4. Cover 12 pages of the middle section with colored or printed paper. Beginning with January, write the name of a month at the top of each page. Decorate each page.

5. Cover 31 pages of the last section with colored or printed paper. Beginning with the number 1, write a number (from 1 to 31) on the top of each page. Decorate each page.

6. Cut a 4 by 5-inch (10 by 13-cm) piece of cardboard. Fold the two longer sides up 1 inch (2.5 cm). Glue the folded edges to the front and back covers. This is the stand for the calendar.

If you are recycling an old notebook, make sure it has at least 31 blank pages. Every morning remember to flip your calendar to the next day!

This quick pillow project is surprisingly comfy!

Small Flowers Pillow

Here is what you need:

green 1-inch-wide
(2.5-cm) ribbon

ruler

3 large bath scrubbies

3 pom-poms

scissors

white craft glue

Here is what you do:

1. Tie the rope loops of the three scrubbies together to secure the scrubbies to one another.

2. Cut two 4-foot (1.2-m) pieces of the ribbon.

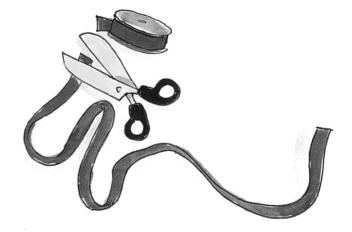

3. Thread the ribbons through the ropes. Tie them in a knot so the ends hang down.

4. Glue a pom-pom in the center of each scrubby to resemble the center of a flower.

This pillow is as pretty as it is comfortable. It will look wonderful displayed on your bed.

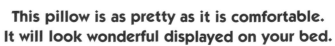

Make an ordinary dresser extraordinary with this easy project!

Dresser Knob Flowers

Here is what you need:

scissors

white craft glue

artificial flowers

Here is what you do:

1. Pull two or three different flowers apart by removing the plastic center to separate the layers of petals.

2. Choose three different petal rounds and stack them to make a new flower.

$3.$ Fold the flower in half. Cut a slit in the center. Fold the flower the opposite way. Cut another slit. This X slit should be big enough to slip over the dresser knob you are placing it on.

$4.$ Line the Xs up. Glue the petal layers together.

$5.$ Cut off two leaves from a flower stem.

$6.$ Glue a leaf on each side of the back of the flower. Be careful not to glue the leaves over the opening. Let dry. Slip the flower over a dresser knob.

Make a different flower for each knob on your dresser. How pretty!

Need a place to stash your pajamas?

Funny Face PJ Bag

Here is what you need:

red and black
felt scraps

heavy red yarn

white craft glue

2 knit hats

scissors

eyelash yarn in 2 colors

a large and a small
pom-pom

Here is what you do:

1. Unfold the rim of one cap to make the head.

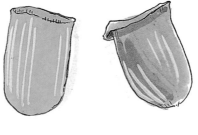

2. Glue the front edge of the head cap inside the front edge of the second hat.

3. Cut eyes from the black felt. Glue them to the head.

4. Glue on a small pom-pom nose and a yarn smile.

5. Cut cheeks from the red felt. Glue them on.

6. Glue eyelash yarn around the inside edge of the hat for hair.

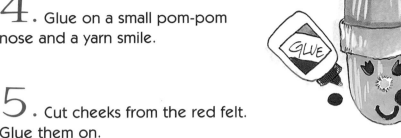

7. Wrap eyelash yarn around your hand 40 times.

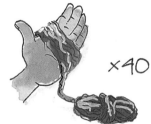

×40

8. Slip the yarn off your hand. Tie a piece of yarn around the center of the loop that has been formed.

9. Spread the yarn out in a circle to look like a flower. Glue a large pom-pom in the center.

10. Glue the flower to the brim of the hat.

Slip your pajamas into the bag through the opening in the back of the hat.

Make this soft little bag to store special jewelry.

Jewelry Pouch

Here is what you need:

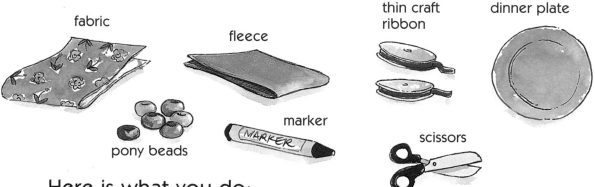

fabric

fleece

thin craft ribbon

dinner plate

pony beads

marker

scissors

Here is what you do:

1. Use the marker to trace around the dinner plate on the back of the fabric. Cut out the circle.

2. Cut out an identical circle from the fleece fabric.

3. Place the fleece circle over the back of the fabric circle. The fleece circle will line the pouch.

4. Fold over 1 inch (2.5 cm) of the two fabrics' edges one section at a time. Cut six slits in each quarter of the circle.

5. Cut two 40-inch (100-cm) pieces of ribbon.

6. Thread one ribbon down through the first slit from the printed side of the pouch. Thread the ribbon in and out through the slits until you are at the last slit.

7. Thread the second ribbon down through the slit on the opposite side of the first ribbon ends. Thread the ribbon in and out of the slits until you come to the last slit.

8. Thread three pony beads on the two ribbons on each side. Knot the ends of the two ribbons together, and trim the ends.

Pull on the ribbons to gather the sides into a bag. Tie the ribbons into a bow to close.

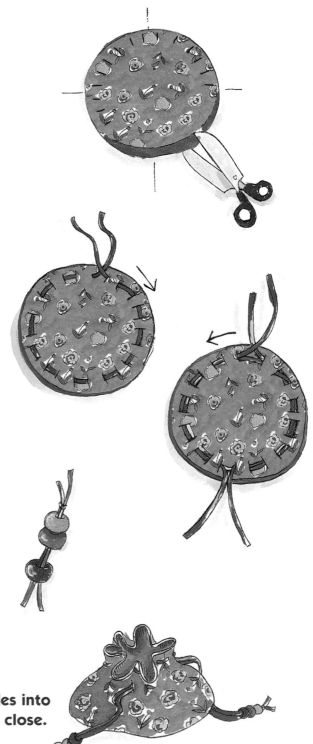

Use these hangers to plan a week's worth of outfits ahead of time.

Days of the Week Hangers

Here is what you need:

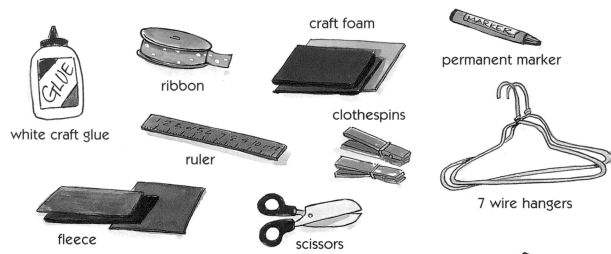

white craft glue

ribbon

craft foam

permanent marker

ruler

clothespins

fleece

scissors

7 wire hangers

Here is what you do:

1. Cut 1-inch-wide (2.5-cm) strips from the fleece. Make them as long as your fabric piece allows.

2. Tie the end of a fleece strip around the neck of a hanger.

3. Wrap the strip around the hanger, including the hanger. If the first strip runs out, secure the end with a dab of glue. Glue the end of a new strip over the end of the strip where you left off and continue wrapping.

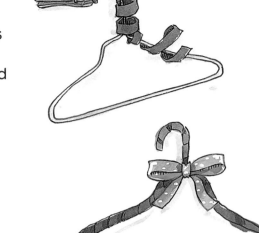

4. Use clothespins to help secure glued ends. Let dry.

5. Tie a ribbon in a bow around the neck of the hanger.

6. Cut a 1½ by 3-inch (3.8 by 8-cm) piece of craft foam. Write a day of the week on the foam.

7. Cut a slit across the top and bottom of the foam. Slide the foam down to the the base of the hook. Make six more hangers for the other days of the week.

Clamp two clothespins to the bottom of some of the hangers to hold skirts and pants.

Decorate your room with a garland of photos!

Friends and Family Photo Garland

Here is what you need:

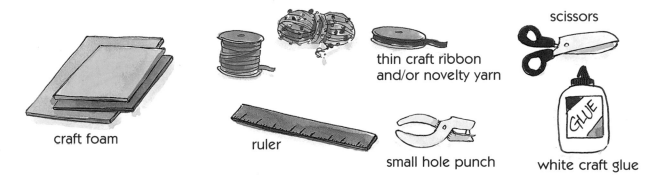

craft foam

ruler

thin craft ribbon and/or novelty yarn

small hole punch

scissors

white craft glue

Here is what you do:

1. Cut two 3 by 4-inch (8 by 10-cm) pieces from one color of craft foam. To make the front of the frame, cut a rectangle from the center of one piece.

2. Make five or more frames from different colors of craft foam.

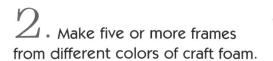

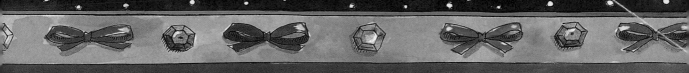

3. Hold the front and back pieces of the frame together. Punch two holes 1 inch (2.5 cm) apart at the top and the bottom of the frames.

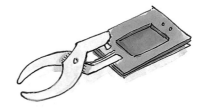

4. Thread ribbon through the bottom holes of the front and back pieces of each frame. Tie the ribbon in a bow.

5. Cut pieces from the foam scraps to make flowers or other decorations for the frames. Glue decorations to each frame.

6. Thread a long piece of thin ribbon or novelty yarn in and out through the holes at the top of each frame to string them together to make the garland.

7. Tie the ribbon or yarn at each end of the garland into a loop for hanging.

Slide a special picture into each frame through the side, and hang the garland up. The pictures can easily be changed.

Post all your important reminders on this project.

Gems Message Can

Here is what you need:

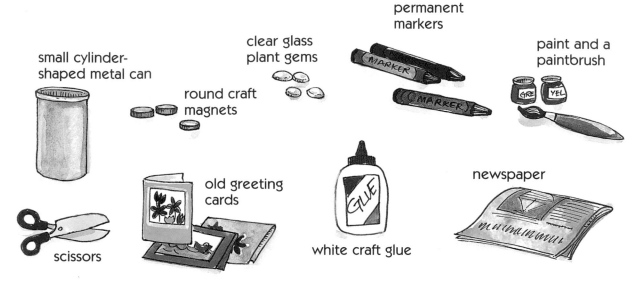

small cylinder-shaped metal can

round craft magnets

clear glass plant gems

permanent markers

paint and a paintbrush

GRE YEL

scissors

old greeting cards

GLUE

white craft glue

newspaper

Here is what you do:

1. Working on the newspaper, paint the outside of the can a light color.

2. Cut pictures of flower heads, birds, and insects the same size as the glass gems.

3. Glue a picture behind each glass gem so it can be seen through the rounded top of the gem.

4. Glue a round magnet to the back of each gem.

5. Use the markers to draw an outdoor scene with flower stems, a tree, and grass on the can.

6. Place the flower heads on the stems, birds in the tree, and insects in the air and grass. Have fun creating a scene with the pictures you use.

Place a pencil and several small squares of scrap paper inside the can to write notes to yourself. Post the notes on the outside of the can using the gem magnets.

Need a way to organize your socks?

Sock Stasher

Here is what you need:

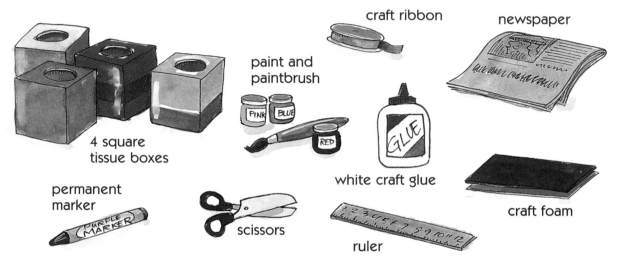

4 square tissue boxes

paint and paintbrush

PINK   BLUE
RED

craft ribbon

newspaper

white craft glue

craft foam

permanent marker

PURPLE MARKER

scissors

ruler

Here is what you do:

1. Glue the four boxes together to form a larger square. Let dry.

2. Trace around the bottom of four glued-together boxes on a piece of craft foam.

3. Cut out the foam.

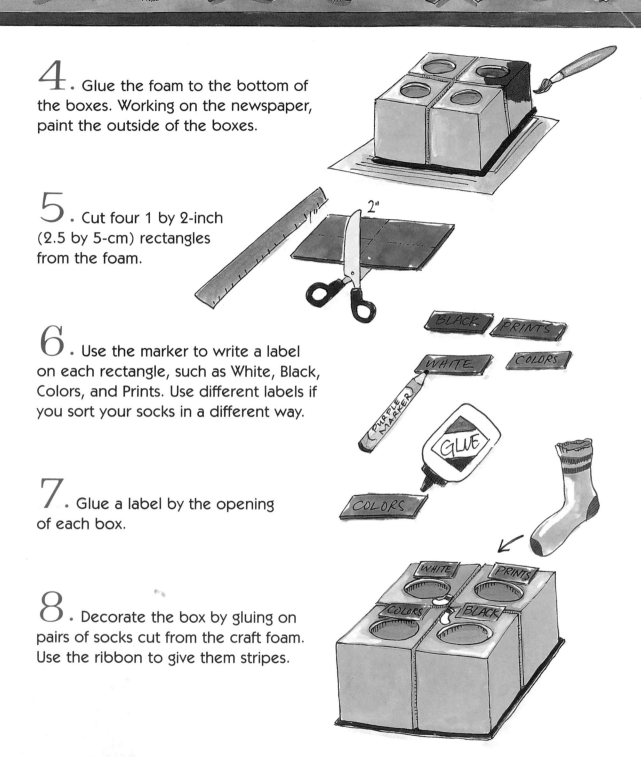

4. Glue the foam to the bottom of the boxes. Working on the newspaper, paint the outside of the boxes.

5. Cut four 1 by 2-inch (2.5 by 5-cm) rectangles from the foam.

6. Use the marker to write a label on each rectangle, such as White, Black, Colors, and Prints. Use different labels if you sort your socks in a different way.

7. Glue a label by the opening of each box.

8. Decorate the box by gluing on pairs of socks cut from the craft foam. Use the ribbon to give them stripes.

Each box will hold several pair of socks. If you have lots of socks, you can add more boxes to your sock stasher. The stasher can be placed flat in a drawer or on its side on a shelf or dresser.

Make pretty letters to spell out your name or a word such as *Joy* or *Giggle!*

Flower Letters

Here is what you need:

single stem
artificial flowers

pipe cleaners or
sparkle stems

multistemmed
artificial flowers

Here is what you do:

1. Choose a multistemmed artificial flower to create the first letter. It does not matter if a few flowers are missing as long as the stems and leaves are still there.

2. Decide on the word you are going to make.

3. Bend the wire flower stems of the multistem bunch of flowers to form the first letter. To hold two flowers together for a letter, just wrap the flowers with a pipe cleaner or sparkle stem.

bend

4. Some letters, such as *H*, may need an additional single stem flower to finish. Attach the additional stem using a pipe cleaner or sparkle stem.

5. To hang a letter, wrap a sparkle stem around your finger. Twist one end around the top of a letter you want to hang. Make more hangers for the rest of the letters.

These letters look wonderful leaning against the back wall of a shelf.

This cute critter will keep track of your spare change.

Caterpillar Bank

Here is what you need:

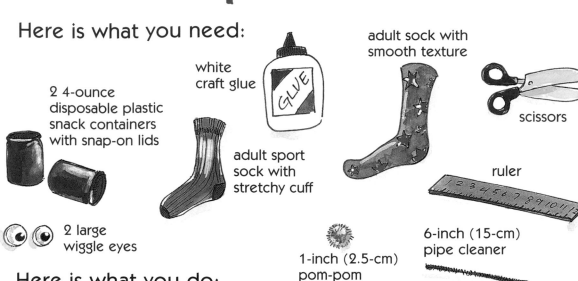

2 4-ounce disposable plastic snack containers with snap-on lids

white craft glue

adult sport sock with stretchy cuff

adult sock with smooth texture

scissors

ruler

2 large wiggle eyes

1-inch (2.5-cm) pom-pom

6-inch (15-cm) pipe cleaner

Here is what you do:

1. Cut a crescent-shape smile out of one of the lids.

2. Glue the pom-pom nose and wiggle eyes above the smile.

3. Bend the pipe cleaner in half and out at the ends to make the tentacles. Glue the base of the tentacles to the top of the head.

4. Cut off the bottoms of both containers. Take off the top lids.

5. Slip a container into the smooth sock, top down.

6. Slip the second container into the sock bottom first, so the two cut bottoms of the containers touch.

7. The top of the sock should just close over the open bottom of the second container.

8. Trim the excess sock from the bottom, leaving ½ inch (1.3-cm) edge. Snap the lid over the bottom container.

9. Snap the face lid over the top container.

10. Cut four 1-inch (2.5-cm) bands from the cuff of the second sock. Slip the bands over the body of the caterpillar to give it stripes.

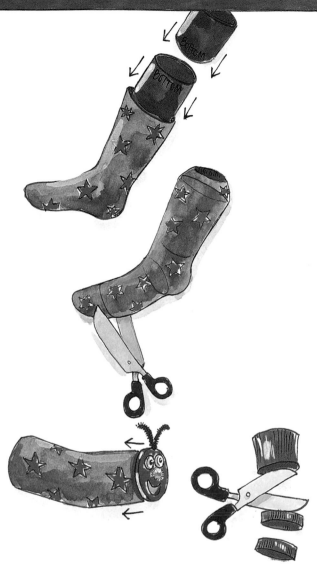

To use the bank, drop coins in through the mouth of the caterpillar. Money can be removed by snapping the lid off the bottom of the bank.

Collect dangling earrings from garage sales,
or use this project to display your own.

Earring Basket

Here is what you need:

dangling earrings

white craft glue

newspaper

2 inexpensive
woven baskets

spray paint or paint
and a paintbrush

scissors

Here is what you do:

1. Cut off the handles
of both baskets.

$2.$ Turn one basket over to become a base for the other basket. Glue the bottoms of the baskets together.

$3.$ Working on newspaper, paint the basket and base in your favorite color. If using spray paint, you may want to ask an adult to help you. Be sure to use a mask and goggles. Let dry.

$4.$ Slip the wire ends of the dangling earrings into the weave around the basket to decorate the basket and display the earrings.

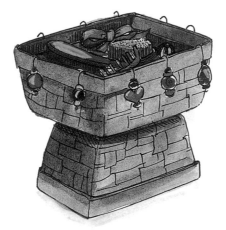

If you are decorating the basket with earrings you don't plan to wear, secure them with a dab of glue.

Make a variety of cute covers for the personal products, such as hairspray, that you keep on your dresser.

Cute Can and Bottle Covers

Here is what you need:

ribbon and/or trim

single sock in pretty color

scissors

ruler

Here is what you do:

1. Find a sock with a stretchy cuff that fits over the container you wish to cover.

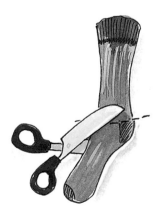

2. Cut off the foot portion of the sock. Make the piece long enough to cover the container.

3224

44

3. Fold over one end of the sock.

4. Cut an even number of ¼-inch (0.6-cm) slits around the edge.

5. Unfold the top of the sock. Weave a piece of ribbon or trim in and out through the slits.

6. Slip the sock over the can so the ribbon end is on top. Tie the ribbon or trim in a pretty bow.

You can weave additional rows of ribbon at the center and bottom of the sock if you wish.

Make this handy table to use when doing projects.

Floor Table

Here is what you need:

paint and paintbrush

newspaper

corrugated box lid

white craft glue

ruler

ribbon

scissors

5 paper towel tubes

12 by 13 by 3-inch (30 by 33 by 8-cm) mailing box

Here is what you do:

1. Turn the box lid so that the flat part becomes a tabletop with the edges hanging down.

2. Decide how high you want the table to be for you. Trim the four tubes to the correct height.

3. Glue a tube to each corner of the bottom of the table. Let dry.

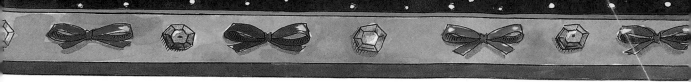

4. Cut off the open end of the mailing box. Glue the box to one side of the table.

5. Cut an 8-inch (20-cm) piece of cardboard tube. Cut the tube in half lengthwise to make a pen and pencil tray. Glue the tray to the edge of the table.

6. Working on the newspaper, paint the table. Let dry.

7. Decorate the table, pen and pencil holder, and side pocket by gluing on strips of ribbon.

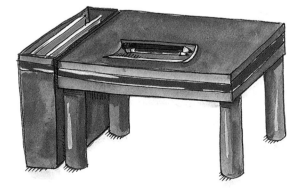

Use your table to write on, stash papers, and hold pencils and pens when doing a project on the floor of your room.

About the Author

With more than one million copies of her books in print, Kathy Ross has written over fifty titles and her name has become synonymous with "top quality craft books." Following twenty five years of developing nursery school programs and guiding young children through craft projects, Ross has authored many successful series, including *Crafts for Kids Who Are Learning about...*, *Girl Crafts*, and *All New Holiday Crafts for Kids*.